OVERVIEW

Overview

Dismissing an employee is never a stress-free task. It can be emotionally daunting and – if done improperly – could have legal ramifications. However, with preparation, you can make this tough experience easier on yourself, your company, and the employee being dismissed.

To make the dismissal process run smoother, there are four steps you can take when considering whether to dismiss an employee. The first is to ensure the employee knows the rules. The second is to warn the employee of inappropriate performance or behavior, and plan corrective actions. The third is to assess the employee's improvement after a given time frame and then make a final decision. The fourth is to prepare a clear and concise dismissal letter, if necessary.

In this course, you'll learn more about the appropriate steps to take prior to dismissing an employee. This includes using documentation to facilitate awareness and following a progressive disciplinary procedure. You'll also find out how to determine if a dismissal is warranted based on the offense, an assessment of the employee, and the organizational impact.

At some point in their careers, most managers will have to undertake the unpleasant task of dismissing an employee. Although this can make for an uncomfortable conversation, both the manager and the employee can learn and grow from the experience if it's handled correctly.

If you feel unsure about how to handle dismissals there are guidelines you can follow that will increase your confidence and make for a smoother experience. Handling dismissals effectively means preserving the dignity of the employee and minimizing the impact on the team and the organization.

You, as a manager, can follow three steps to managing dismissals effectively. This course outlines the steps involved in preparing for dismissals; guidelines for conducting a dismissal interview, such as dealing with employee reactions; and what to consider when following up on the dismissal after the meeting.

CHAPTER 1 - PREPARING TO DISMISS AN EMPLOYEE

CHAPTER 1 - Preparing to Dismiss an Employee
   SECTION 1 - Benefits of Preparing to Dismiss an Employee
   SECTION 2 - Warning the Employee
   SECTION 3 - Making a Final Decision
   SECTION 4 - Preparing a Dismissal Letter

SECTION 1 - BENEFITS OF PREPARING TO DISMISS AN EMPLOYEE

SECTION 1 - Benefits of Preparing to Dismiss an Employee

By properly preparing for employee dismissals, you can overcome such obstacles as fear, becoming too emotionally involved, and legal threats. Proper preparation for dismissal includes not only following a progressive disciplinary procedure, but providing just cause, as well as treating all employees fairly and consistently for similar conduct.

You might have to dismiss employees for inappropriate behavior or performance failure – or a combination of both. The first step in tackling the situation is to alert employees to the issues. It's also important to use documentation such as employee handbooks, job descriptions, and performance reviews. That way, you not only make the problems clear to employees, but the documentation helps support just cause for dismissal if that proves to be necessary.

BENEFITS OF DISMISSAL PREPARATION

Benefits of dismissal preparation

Dismissing an employee properly means handling the situation so it reduces risk. Possible risks include lawsuits, decreases in morale and productivity, theft, and escalated incidents in dismissal interviews.

There are three reasons managers often put off dismissing employees: fear of the unknown, emotional involvement with employees, and possible legal consequences.

Fear

Perhaps you've never dismissed an employee before. You may not know exactly what to expect or how to handle it. Or maybe you've had a bad experience dismissing an employee in the past.

Whatever the case, there are people within your company whom you can turn to. First of all, you should talk to HR about the proper dismissal process at your company. You can also ask other managers for advice and even sit in on an employee dismissal as a witness. That way, you can learn more about employee reactions and how to handle them.

Emotional involvement

It can be especially difficult to dismiss employees you've made a connection with. People you have to dismiss may be your friends. They may have families to support and bills to pay. In short, they're human and so are you.

However, you've got to keep in mind dismissals are not personal; they're a part of doing business. At the same time, you shouldn't lose your compassion. It's in these times that your employees will really appreciate it. They should leave the dismissal feeling as though they'd been given a fair chance.

Legal consequences

Former employees can sue a company for wrongful dismissal if there's no just cause for the dismissal. Maybe you've even experienced a lawsuit firsthand. It's not inevitable though. In fact, if you're following dismissal procedures properly, chances are you've got yourself covered legally.

Consider this scenario where a manager didn't follow the proper process for dismissing an employee. Spence is a first-time manager of a production line team at a manufacturing facility. For several months he's had difficulty with his employee, Nicole, regarding her work hours.

The problems started when Nicole was late for work a few times and didn't call ahead. When Spence brought it up casually, Nicole explained that her daughter had been sick. She promised that once her daughter started feeling well, she'd be in on time.

Spence thought Nicole's explanation was valid and that the situation would only be temporary. He actually felt embarrassed that he'd questioned her, so he didn't bother writing up the incidents.

As time passed, Nicole began to arrive at work later and later every day. This left the production line short an essential worker and impacted productivity. Spence had to call in temporary workers on more than one occasion – and he even took over Nicole's role himself once. She'd missed more hours than she actually had in sick days.

Still, Spence was afraid to approach Nicole. First of all, he liked her as a person and didn't want to upset her. He also knew that she was a single mother providing the only source of income for her family. In addition, he'd never actually dismissed an employee before. He was worried about what to expect – emotionally and legally.

One day, Nicole didn't show up for work. It was on this day that the CEO visited to check on the production lines. Spence was furious. When Nicole came in the following day, Spence dismissed her harshly and immediately in front of her coworkers. He didn't give her an opportunity to explain herself, but told her to leave before he did "more than just hurt her feelings."

Soon after the incident, Nicole filed several lawsuits against the company. She claimed Spence told her to take as much time as she needed until her daughter got better. Although this wasn't exactly the case, Spence couldn't back up his side of the story because he never formally noted the incidents. Plus, while his threat in the heat of the moment wasn't serious, Nicole took it that way.

In this scenario, the company could've avoided Nicole's lawsuits if a progressive disciplinary procedure was followed. Progressive discipline focuses on deterring employees from repeating unwanted behavior by providing incremental warnings before dismissal. This means that employees have the chance to fix reported problems immediately and avoid potential dismissal. And it also means that employers can prove just cause.

Dismissing an Employee

For example, Spence should've given Nicole a clear verbal warning about her tardiness as a first corrective action – explaining the consequences.

The second step that Spence should've taken was to review documented company rules about being on time and family sick leave. Nicole would've been provided with this information at the start of her employment, but she should have been required to reread it.

She should've then been given the opportunity to ask questions before signing formal documentation acknowledging her understanding of the rules.

Besides lack of progressive discipline, there are two other main reasons companies may lose employee lawsuits. First, if the company doesn't have policies outlining grounds for dismissal, it may seem that the company is dismissing an employee without just cause. Second, if the company doesn't apply discipline fairly – such as treating similar cases differently - it may seem that one employee is getting preferential treatment. These reasons are why it's important to coordinate with HR when dealing with legal considerations.

Following proper steps to dismiss an employee may give you the confidence needed to make it go as smoothly as possible – if it's actually required. Sometimes giving the employee an opportunity to correct the situation will make dismissal unnecessary. If this isn't the case and you still have to dismiss the employee, you've given the person a chance and you've followed procedure. This should put any fears you have about the dismissal to rest, including emotional and legal concerns.

Question

What are some benefits of appropriate preparation for dismissing an employee?

Options:

1. Overcoming the fear of what to expect when dismissing an employee
2. Avoiding lawsuits the employee may file against the company
3. Being fair to the employee by giving the person chances to improve and correct the situation
4. Maintaining the friendship with the employee being dismissed
5. Being able to dismiss an employee in such a way that strong emotion is removed from the equation

Answer

Option 1: This option is correct. While you can never know with certainty an employee's reaction during a dismissal, you can anticipate common outcomes. You can also control how you handle yourself – which may alleviate some anxiety.

Option 2: This option is correct. If you follow progressive disciplinary procedures, you'll probably have just cause for an employee dismissal.

Option 3: This option is correct. Employees can't improve at their jobs if they're unaware of the issues. When you tell them what's expected, they might just correct the problems, leaving no reason for dismissal.

Option 4: This option is incorrect. Being sensitive to the employee during a dismissal is important. However, dismissals aren't focused on friendships.

Option 5: This option is incorrect. Dismissals should be kept professional. This includes being sensitive to the employee.

KEEPING EMPLOYEES INFORMED

Keeping employees informed

The correct process when determining whether to dismiss an employee involves four steps. First, make sure the employee knows the rules and what is expected. Second, warn the employee and plan corrective actions. Third, make a final decision after the employee has had opportunity to improve over a given time frame. And fourth, prepare the dismissal letter.

The first step in the process is to make sure the employee knows the rules and what is expected. Otherwise, you risk exposing your company to lawsuits. Employees need to know how to behave or perform in their roles so they can do what's required of them.

Two common reasons for dismissing employees are behavior problems and performance issues. An example of a behavior problem is when an employee continually makes long personal calls at work despite company policy.

An example of a performance issue is when an employee regularly fails to meet sales targets. These two kinds of reasons can exist separately or together. Whichever is the case, employees should be made aware of where they are going wrong.

Even when the rules and expectations seem intuitive or clear from verbal communication, it's still necessary to also provide documentation. Places where employees can find such information include employee handbooks, job descriptions, and performance reviews.

Employee handbooks

Every company should have an employee handbook. It provides employees with written information on company policies that must be followed, as well as the consequences of failing to do so. It includes information on expected employee conduct. It should be given to employees when they start at the company. Managers should request they read it, ask any questions they may have about it, and then sign it to verify they've understood it.

Copies of signed employee handbooks should be kept in personnel files. While an employee handbook is not a contract with employees, it does serve as a conduct guide. Having employees sign it may make it easier to clarify reasons for dismissal.

Job descriptions

When a candidate applies for a job, a description of the role is usually given. It outlines the performance expectations of the particular position. However, this description can still be useful after the hiring process. A job description gives the employee a guide for performing a job according to the requirements of the company. It also provides the company with documentation to refer to if the employee is to be dismissed.

Performance reviews

Performance reviews measure the extent that employees have been meeting their set performance targets. Feedback is provided to help employees improve in their jobs.

A copy of a sample performance review document should be included in the employee handbook. That way, employees will know what to expect.

Consider this scenario where a manager addresses the behavior and underperformance of an employee. Larry has been working as a mechanic in a truck and trailer service shop for over four years. In the past, he's been commended not only for his excellent customer service, but for his quality and speed of work. Customers were asking for him specifically.

However, over the past three months, Larry's manager, Shelley, has noticed a change in his attitude and performance. He has started to tell customers that he's too busy to work on their vehicles or that the issues are beyond his expertise. Based on past performance, Shelley is certain this isn't the case.

Company policy requires Shelley to conduct a performance review when an employee has not been meeting expectations for a period of two months or more.

Follow along as Shelley conducts a performance review with Larry.

Shelley: Thank you for meeting with me. How are things going?

Shelley greets Larry with a welcoming tone and a smile.

Larry: They've been better. My wife is still trying to find a job. It's been really difficult making ends meet on just one salary.

Larry is sad.

Shelley: I can empathize with that. I'm sure Emily will find something soon. In the meantime, I want you to know that your hard work and skill set is appreciated here. However, over these past few months, you're not performing as usual. I'm concerned about that.

Shelley is empathetic and genuine.

Larry: Is it that I'm not meeting my service targets?

Larry is concerned.

Shelley: That's part of it. Let's take a look at your figures over the last three months. You can see that you are performing well below the minimum levels that were outlined in your job description.

Shelley points to a document and talks seriously.

Larry: Wow. I didn't think I was doing that poorly. What was the other thing you were concerned about?

Larry is genuinely surprised.

Shelley: You're not providing the customer service that's expected. As a part of our company policy, you need to interact in a helpful and friendly way to clients and coworkers alike.

Shelley is speaking seriously.

Larry: I know, I know. I've just lost my way a bit. Sorry for that. I'll improve.

Larry is apologetic.

Shelley: I'm certain you will. And in order to help you do that I'd like you to work with a mentor and attend customer service training. Then we'll check in a month to see how things are going. How does that sound?

Shelley is positive and genuine.

Larry: OK.

Larry is in agreement.

Shelley: Good! If you don't have any questions about this review, could you please sign off on this document that outlines what we've discussed? I'll make sure you get a copy for your records.

Shelley is positive and genuine.

Question

Katerina is an employee who requires an Internet connection to help her do her job. However, reports on Internet usage over a two-month period have shown that she's been using it to conduct personal business and for entertainment purposes during nonworking hours. Although it hasn't yet affected her work performance, Katerina's conduct is clearly against company policy.

Which statements describe appropriate actions her manager should take to ensure Katerina knows what's expected of her?

Options:

1. Meet with her privately to discuss the Internet issue, as well as the consequences of continued misuse

2. Ask her to reread the section of the employee handbook that details company policy on Internet usage and then get her to sign it

3. Go over her job description and ask her if there is anything in it that she doesn't understand

4. Conduct a mini performance review based upon her misuse of the Internet

Answer

Option 1: This option is correct. In order for Katerina to improve upon her behavior, she must be made aware of it. It's essential that she understands what actions will be taken if the issue isn't resolved.

Option 2: This option is correct. The employee handbook provides information on company policies, such as Internet usage. Katerina has probably been asked to sign this when she first received it. However, it's important to document that she's reread it.

Option 3: This option is incorrect. In this case, the problem is not Katerina's job performance – it's her behavior. The employee handbook is more likely to detail company policies.

Option 4: This option is incorrect. Performance reviews usually deal with performance rather than behavior.

SECTION 2 - WARNING THE EMPLOYEE

SECTION 2 - Warning the Employee

Employees in danger of dismissal need to know their offenses so they can take action to change their behavior. Progressive discipline also provides documentation that helps support just cause in the case of dismissal.

Minor offenses are those that cause no immediate harm, but can be disruptive and lead to larger problems. When employees commit minor offenses, your company's progressive disciplinary procedure should be followed. This usually consists of first providing a verbal warning, followed by at least one written warning. You may also want to consider providing employees that commit minor offenses with training or mentoring. If this doesn't work, then the next step is to consider dismissal. You may choose to suspend the employee while you make your final decision.

On the other hand, major offenses hurt people or the company. Major offenses can be physical, emotional, or intellectual in nature. There's typically no tolerance for such offenses and the result is usually immediate dismissal.

SEVERITY OF OFFENSES

Severity of offenses

Once you've ensured your employee is aware of the behavior or performance issue, the next step toward dismissal is to take disciplinary actions. Major offenses such as theft usually warrant immediate dismissal. Minor offenses like taking unauthorized breaks are likely cases for progressive discipline and corrective actions. In such cases, failure of the employee to comply could lead to dismissal.

Employee handbooks usually outline what constitutes major and minor offenses. There are also different rules and regulations according to your location. When in doubt, consult your HR Department. However, a good rule of thumb is that if employees are endangering others, themselves, or the company and its property willfully, the offense is probably major. Examples of offenses that are often classified as major include dishonesty, gross negligence, intoxication, insolence, fighting, safety violations, and breaching confidentiality clauses.

On the other hand, minor offenses are miscellaneous performance or behavior-related issues that are not immediately harmful, but can be disruptive and lead to bigger problems.

For example, imagine an employee who continually refuses to follow your instructions. There comes a point when dealing with the same issue from this employee can become frustrating to everyone in the work environment. Not only that, but the employee's behavior could be affecting the company's productivity or stability.

If that employee continues to be insubordinate and difficult to work with, failure to address the issue could lead to further problems. For example, the company's major project might not be completed on time or budget. Or the employee's level of insubordination could increase, leading to a major offense.

Examples of minor offenses include incompetence, excessive absences or lateness, smoking in unauthorized areas, unauthorized breaks, minor insubordination, and failure to report to work.

Question

Match the offense to its severity. Each severity may have more than one match.

Options:

A. Poor performance on work assignments
B. Smoking in unauthorized areas
C. Stealing money from the company
D. Having lied about credentials when applying for the job

Targets:

1. Minor offense
2. Major offense

Answer

Minor offenses like poor work performance and smoking in unauthorized areas usually don't cause immediate harm. However, if they're continued, they can cause frustration and lead to bigger issues.

Major offenses like theft and dishonesty can cause immediate harm to employees or the company.

HOW TO HANDLE OFFENSES

How to handle offenses

There are different types of actions to take depending on the severity of the offense. Major offenses often warrant immediate dismissal, whereas minor offenses usually require progressive discipline and corrective actions. This allows employees the opportunity to correct the performance or behavior in question. If they're able to do this, there's no need for dismissal. However, if employees fail to improve after progressive discipline and corrective actions, there's potential for dismissal.

Progressive discipline is a system where the severity of the disciplinary action increases in relation to the nature and continuation of the offense. This allows employees the chance to correct minor offenses to avoid dismissal. There are three types of progressive discipline measures that come before dismissal: verbal warning, written warning, and suspension.

Verbal warning

A verbal warning is typically the first time the employee has been alerted to the minor offense. The verbal warning should be clear, state corrective requirements, and give consequences for failure to comply. Best practice is to document what happened during the verbal warning for your files.

Written warning

A written warning is issued when the verbal warning does not lead to an improvement in behavior or performance. A written warning formally documents the time, place, and date of the incident, as well as the people present and the organizational impact. Companies provide information on the number of written warnings required before moving to the next step of the progressive disciplinary procedure. Your company manual should specify this. If not, consult HR.

Written warnings should be signed by the employee and the manager, and a copy should be kept on file. Written warnings usually stay on an employee's record with the company for up to a year. If the employee refuses to sign the written warning, have a witness sign it. The witness should indicate that the employee received the written warning. Then give a copy of the signed warning to the employee.

Suspension

After progressive discipline and corrective actions have failed, in most cases the final step before dismissal should be suspension. The suspension of an employee serves many purposes. First, it signals that the employee's job is in jeopardy. It also allows the company and the employee time to further evaluate the situation. Sometimes during a suspension, especially one that is unpaid, an employee may simply decide to quit before potential dismissal. Suspensions can last days or weeks depending on the situation.

Progressive discipline usually calls for corrective actions. Where applicable, employees should be given the opportunity to improve their behavior or performance issues. This could include providing them with a coach or mentor to help ensure they know what's expected of them. There are also instances where training or retraining could assist with problems. Whichever is the case, you should document all corrective actions that are suggested, taken, or refused.

Question

Place the steps for progressive discipline in the case of a minor employee offense in the correct order.

Options:
A. Verbal warning
B. Written warning
C. Suspension
D. Dismissal

Answer

Verbal warning is ranked Step one. The first step in a progressive discipline procedure is usually a verbal warning. This alerts the employee that there is an issue.

Written warning is ranked Step two. The second step in a progressive discipline procedure is usually a written warning. A written warning typically follows a verbal warning.

Suspension is ranked Step three. The third step in a progressive discipline procedure is suspension. It should be the last option before dismissal.

Dismissal is ranked Step four. The fourth and final step in a progressive discipline procedure is dismissal.

Larry is a truck and trailer mechanic who hasn't been meeting service targets or dealing with customers properly. His manager, Shelley, has met with him for a performance review to let him know about these issues. They agreed to meet again in a month's time to discuss Larry's efforts.

However, even before their next scheduled meeting, Shelley has to give Larry a verbal warning about his behavior and performance. While he's meeting service level targets, he has refused to work with the mentor assigned to him and complete the suggested training. He has also stopped communicating with customers – an essential part of his job.

Follow along as Shelley gives Larry a verbal warning about his behavior.

Shelley: Thank you for meeting with me again. I'd like to discuss your recent behavior and performance issues.

Shelley is serious, but pleasant.

Larry: I thought my service figures were back to expectations.

Larry is confused.

Shelley: They are. I'd like to commend you for that. You were able to take the feedback given during the performance review and apply it to your service levels. However, I need to talk to you about your refusal to go ahead with suggested corrective actions from the performance review.

Shelley is genuine and serious.

Larry: I can't work with Victor – the mentor you assigned me. And I think it's silly that I have to take a course on improving my customer service skills. I've been doing this job for over four years. I think I know how to handle people.

Shelley: I appreciate your concerns. However, recent observations, as well as reports from coworkers indicate that you're not communicating well with customers. Your job description says you're expected to interact with them in a way that is friendly and helpful.

Shelley is direct with Larry while remaining pleasant.

Shelley: Company policy also reiterates the importance of communication. The mentoring and training will help you do your job as required. If your interaction with others doesn't improve, you're at risk for potential dismissal.

Shelley continues to be direct, but pleasant.

Larry: I'm aware of that. I'll attend the training, but I'm not working with Victor. He doesn't want me working here.

Larry is upset.

Shelley: Thanks for agreeing to the training. I'm planning on going with you to show my support. Still, it's very important for you to work with a mentor. I don't understand your concerns about Victor. You should be able to work with him. However, I'll allow you to work with Rosa Gomez as your mentor instead.

Shelley is genuine and pleasant.

Larry: Thank you. I can work with Rosa.

Larry is content with Shelley's response.

Dismissing an Employee

Shelley: Great! I'm so glad that we discussed this. I'm going to make a note about our conversation for the company records. Please let me know if I can help you further with your efforts to improve your work performance.

Shelley is content with Larry's response.

On the first day of scheduled training, Larry is absent. Shelley consults the company's policy manual to see what she should do. It states that managers give employees two written warnings before suspension or dismissal for minor offenses.

Shelley feels that she has no other choice but to give Larry a first written warning to highlight the seriousness of the situation. She asks her manager to sit in on this next part of the progressive disciplinary procedure with Larry.

This first written warning Shelley gives to Larry refers to both the past performance review and the verbal warning. It also restates what Larry needs to do to improve his behavior and performance. Shelley goes over it thoroughly with Larry and asks if he has any questions. Although Larry is aware of the consequences of not meeting these expectations, he refuses to sign the warning.

Question

In the scenario featuring Larry and Shelley, Larry refuses to sign his first written warning.

What should Shelley do?

Options:

1. Shelley should get her manager to sign the written warning as a witness. Then she should give a copy to Larry and keep one for the company's records.

2. Shelley should immediately give Larry a second written warning for minor insubordination. Then she should give him a copy of both written warnings.

3. Shelley's should get her manager to intervene in the progressive discipline by making Larry sign the written warning as a condition of his employment.

4. Shelley should dismiss Larry immediately while her manager acts as a witness. Then she should send Larry all applicable paperwork by mail.

Answer

Option 1: This is the correct option. Employees may sometimes refuse to sign off on written warnings. In such cases, these actions should be noted and witnessed.

Option 2: This option is incorrect. A second written warning is not warranted in this case. However, Shelley should give Larry a copy of any paperwork that comes from disciplinary actions.

Option 3: This option is incorrect. Larry shouldn't be threatened into signing the written warning. If Larry doesn't sign it, a note about his refusal to sign off will be witnessed by Shelley's manager and then put in Larry's personnel file.

Option 4: This option is incorrect. Dismissal is not warranted here. The correct thing to do is to get the witness to sign notations on what happened. A copy of this documentation will be given to Larry and one will be kept on file.

Not long after this first written warning, Larry stops working with his mentor. He tells Shelley that he won't let the company treat him like a child anymore.

At this point, Shelley writes Larry's second and final warning. It reiterates that Larry is being given an opportunity to improve. It provides a required action plan and a time line to make improvements. It states that Larry has 30 days to comply with expectations.

When Larry gets a copy of this second written warning, he recognizes he's in danger of dismissal if his improper behavior continues. He signs it and promises to do what's required to keep his position in the company.

Question

Match examples of offenses with the appropriate disciplinary actions. Each offense may match to more than one disciplinary action.

Options:

A. An employee is caught smoking in an unauthorized area for the first time

B. An employee has failed to meet sales targets even after a verbal warning

C. An employee has willfully destroyed the company's photocopier in a bout of anger

D. An employee has repeatedly taken unauthorized breaks, even after progressive discipline

Targets:

1. Verbal warning
2. Written warning
3. Training or coaching
4. Dismissal

Answer

A verbal warning is usually the first step in a progressive discipline procedure that deals with minor offenses like smoking in an unauthorized area for the first time.

A written warning usually follows a verbal warning in a progressive disciplinary procedure that deals with minor offenses. In this case, an employee has already received a verbal warning about substandard performance. So this second warning is one that is written.

Corrective actions are usually suggested for employees when their behavior or performance could benefit from specific training or coaching. Here, the employee could use corrective actions to help with substandard performance.

Dismissal should be immediate for major offenses that cause harm to the employee, coworkers, or the company and its property such as willfully destroying the company's photocopier. In the case of minor offenses like taking unauthorized breaks, dismissal should follow after progressive discipline has failed.

SECTION 3 - MAKING A FINAL DECISION

SECTION 3 - Making a Final Decision

Making the decision to dismiss an employee isn't an easy one. It requires time, due process, and good judgment. In the end, the decision is based on an assessment of the employee and of the organizational impact of the dismissal.

Employees should be assessed in terms of two main criteria: their efforts and their impact on productivity. Negative results in either area can be a reason for dismissal.

The potential impact on the organization also plays a big part in the decision. There may be instances where employees are kept not because of any positive assessment, but because of the circumstances in which the company finds itself.

ASSESSING THE EMPLOYEE

Assessing the employee

The decision to dismiss an employee should only be made after the progressive disciplinary procedure has been followed. The employee should be given a time frame to take the necessary steps to improve. Your conclusion will depend on an assessment of the employee and of the potential impact the dismissal could have on your company.

When assessing an employee for dismissal, you should analyze the individual in terms of behavior, skills, performance, problems, and potential. Keep two general considerations in mind. The first is how the retention or dismissal of this employee would impact productivity. The second is the amount of effort the employee has made to improve. Ask yourself, "Is the employee meeting expectations – or at least trying?"

Consider Larry, a truck and trailer mechanic who is in danger of dismissal. His manager, Shelley, has given him a verbal warning and two written warnings regarding his continued minor offenses.

The written warning included a performance improvement plan. It specifically stated the changes Larry needed to make to keep his job. It included working with a mentor, attending training, and improving customer service scores. Larry was given 30 days to make these changes.

Now that Larry's final assessment date is drawing near, Shelley has a lot to think about. She's never dismissed an employee before and wants to be sure she makes the right decision.

Shelley is going to consider Larry's behavior, skills, performance, problems, and potential. The two critical factors she will consider are Larry's impact on productivity and his efforts to improve. She makes note of these to help her make a more accurate assessment.

Impact on productivity

Larry continues to meet his service targets. However, his customer service scores haven't improved. He falls just short of reaching company standards.

In addition, one coworker asked for a shift change specifically because he didn't want to work with Larry. He said Larry emitted a 'negative energy' that wasn't good for productivity. When I looked at service numbers, I found that the productivity of Larry's coworkers decreased when they worked on the same shift as him. This will have an effect on the company's bottom line.

Efforts to improve

While Larry did work with his mentor, Rosa, she reported that he only did the bare minimum of what was required. I observed the two of them in action and noted that the pairing wasn't ideal.

Larry attended the customer service training with me. I noticed that he didn't participate during the course and seemed not to be listening. Larry scored 85% on the final exam – the exact passing mark.

Larry continued to meet service targets, but never achieved the same levels as before. In addition, his customer service and peer review ratings were just below standards – although he did improve somewhat overall.

From her employee assessment, Shelley finds Larry has improved in some areas. However, even with these positive changes, he still falls slightly short of expectations. She has also observed that Larry hasn't put in his best efforts. Shelley has found that while Larry is meeting prescribed service targets, he's negatively affecting the service figures of others on his shift. Plus, his customer service ratings are still below expectations outlined in the second written warning.

Shelley doubts Larry will change for the better no matter how much time he's given. She feels that she's given him an opportunity to show improvement and he hasn't taken full advantage of it. Shelley decides that Larry's dismissal is necessary. She confirms her decision with her manager. He agrees it's the best thing for the company.

Question

Valerie, an award-winning legal assistant for a small law firm, has been having some noticeable issues in her job. She's misplaced important files and has passed along incorrect or incomplete messages. In addition, she was caught playing computer games when she was supposed to be doing research.

After receiving a verbal warning, Valerie has stopped playing games on the computer and has contributed to a winning major case. However, she still forgets things and delivers wrong information if she doesn't write it down. For example, the other day, she didn't make a call to a client as requested and that person decided to use another law firm that would be "more attentive to his legal needs." After a first written warning, Valerie has purchased a planner for herself and some sticky notes.

Which statements correctly assess Valerie?

Options:

1. Valerie doesn't seem to be intentionally misplacing files or getting messages wrong, but she still cost the firm a client
2. Valerie is an award winner who can potentially help the firm with cases if she's able to focus
3. Valerie isn't willing to improve and her behavior has become costly for the law firm
4. Valerie has put a great amount of energy into fixing the highlighted issues, but this hasn't been reflected in her performance

Answer

Option 1: This option is correct. Valerie has good intentions and has been making some efforts to improve. At the same time, the firm has lost a client due to her substandard performance.

Option 2: This option is correct. Valerie has a proven track record for high performance, so the potential for improvement in terms of productivity is there. She has also made an effort to improve.

Option 3: This option is incorrect. Valerie has made efforts to change her behavior. She stopped playing computer games and she plans to write down messages to avoid forgetfulness and miscommunication. While Valerie caused the loss of a client, her impact on productivity isn't costly, as she also contributed to winning a major case.

Option 4: This option is incorrect. Valerie has put a reasonable amount of effort into improving the highlighted issues.

ASSESSING THE ORGANIZATIONAL IMPACT

Assessing the organizational impact

Another important factor in making your final decision is the potential impact the dismissal may have on your company. A negative employee assessment doesn't necessarily mean a dismissal is imminent. While an employee may not be meeting expectations, there are times when your company has no other choice but to keep the employee – if only temporarily.

There are several reasons you might hesitate to dismiss an employee. First of all, the company could be going through a period of instability. Second, the employee might have a skill set that can't easily be replaced. Third, the manager in charge of the employee is leaving the company and would be leaving the replacement manager with a gap in staff.

Company going through instability

There may be times when a company is going through a period of instability where it wouldn't make sense to dismiss an employee. Say the truck and trailer shop where Larry and Shelley work is undergoing major restructuring. People are being moved to new positions and new teams are being built.

It probably wouldn't be a good time for Shelley to dismiss Larry. The future of her team and the direction of the company are unknown. She probably wouldn't want to find and train someone to replace Larry during such a time of confusion. She mightn't even know what skill set to hire for because of all of the organizational uncertainty.

Skill set can't easily be replaced

Sometimes an employee has a highly-valued skill set that would require too much time or money to replace. In such cases, it might be more beneficial to the company to keep an employee in danger of dismissal.

Say Larry is the only person at the truck and trailer shop who's able to service a particular type of vehicle. Perhaps doing this work is essential to daily business. Even if Shelley thinks it would be best to dismiss him, it might be difficult to find a replacement for Larry. The skill set could be rare. It could take time and money to find a replacement that the company just doesn't have.

Manager leaving the company

A manager in charge of an employee in danger of dismissal may leave the organization for one reason or another. When this happens, it's best that the manager keep the employee. This ensures the replacing manager doesn't have to immediately fill a gap that may affect organizational performance. The decision to dismiss employees can always be made at a later time.

Say Shelley decides to leave her position as manager in the truck and trailer shop. While she planned on dismissing Larry, she mightn't want to leave a gap in the service staff for her replacement to fill. It can be a burden to start a new management job with an incomplete team. The new manager could decide how to handle the dismissal situation with Larry based on the documentation Shelley has completed.

Question

Shirley is a tour guide for a sightseeing company. Her customer service ratings during the off-season were poor. Feedback suggested that she lacked enthusiasm and that she discussed "the dullest historical points imaginable." Shirley's manager, Dave, talked to her about this before, so he felt he had to give her a more formal written warning to show her the seriousness of the situation. It included a performance improvement plan to take place over the slower season.

Shirley's performance doesn't improve during the time frame allotted and it is now peak season. Dave is promoted to another job within the company and has to decide whether to keep or dismiss Shirley before his replacement takes over. While he doesn't know who's getting his job, he's guessing that his replacement could find a university or college student who's off for the summer and wouldn't mind doing Shirley's job.

Based on the scenario, should Dave keep or dismiss Shirley?

Options:
1. Keep
2. Dismiss

Answer

Option 1: This is the correct option. Shirley's performance falls below expectations, but Dave is being promoted to another position. It's probably best that he keep her on staff. That way he won't be leaving his replacement with a gap in the tour operations team during peak season.

Option 2: This is the incorrect option. While Shirley's not meeting her performance expectations, Dave shouldn't dismiss her. He's being promoted to another position and it would be unfair to leave his replacement with a gap in the tour operations team – especially during the peak season.

TIMING AND PERSONAL CONSIDERATIONS

Timing and personal considerations

Once you've decided to dismiss an employee, you should take a day or two to think about what you're about to do. It's a decision not to be taken lightly. During this time you may want to reread documentation on the employee. You may also want to discuss your decision with HR and your superiors. If your conclusion is still the same, dismiss the employee promptly. This will make the dismissal easier for both you and the employee.

There may be instances where you might want to delay dismissing the employee because of personal circumstances. The decision to do so is not clear cut. You'll have to consider each situation individually and decide what's best.

Remember Shelley and Larry? Shelley has already decided to dismiss Larry. However, Larry's wife is currently out of work and a major holiday is fast approaching. For these reasons, Shelley delays the dismissal by a week. She thinks the dismissal may be too much for him to handle during the holiday period. Plus, his offenses aren't affecting the safety of others.

It's human to want to show compassion and support to others during their times of need. However, there comes a point when the company's interests must prevail. It's unreasonable to keep an employee who is negatively impacting productivity and has shown no effort to improve, despite the warnings.

A prompt but sensitive dismissal is best for all parties involved. A delayed dismissal sends a message that the performance or behavior issue is acceptable. This can not only influence productivity, but can make just cause questionable.

Case Study: Question 1 of 3
Scenario

Juan is a veteran photographer for a fashion magazine and has been popular with clients. Recently, his manager, Darlene, started to notice his style of photography was changing. His new photos were not to clients' tastes. They wanted him to take photos reminiscent of the style he became known for. Darlene gave Juan a verbal warning and two written warnings about his performance. Juan was required to revert to his old style of photography and was assigned to a mentor to help him do so. The last written warning stipulated he improve his performance for the magazine's next issue. Juan agreed to all requests.

When the next issue was published, most clients remained dissatisfied with Juan's photos. They decided to take their business elsewhere. Juan told Darlene that the dissatisfaction was due to ignorance; that people didn't understand the new "statement" he was making. Darlene didn't want to dismiss Juan, as such skilled photographers are not easy to come by. However, she had a few up-and-coming photographers on the team who could take over with a little time and training for half of Juan's salary.

Answer the questions in order.

Question

Which statements correctly assess Juan?

Options:

1. Juan isn't willing to revert to his old style of photography and this has caused some clients to take their business elsewhere

2. Juan thinks his current style of photography is making a statement and that clients who don't like it are ignorant

3. Juan has changed his style of photography as per request and some clients have come back

4. Juan took advantage of the corrective actions and his efforts were reflected in the magazine's most recent issue

Answer

Option 1: This option is correct. Juan had potential to revert to his old style of photography and a mentor to help him. However, he refused to change.

Option 2: This option is correct. Juan didn't put effort into reverting to his old style. Instead, he blamed his loss of clients on their unwillingness to change, rather than his.

Option 3: This option is incorrect. Juan was asked to revert to the style that he was originally known for. He didn't. The magazine's clients were largely unimpressed with his efforts.

Option 4: This option is incorrect. Juan did work with a mentor, but still his photos weren't in the same style he previously used. Most clients remained dissatisfied with the magazine's most recent issue.

Case Study: Question 2 of 3

Dismissing an Employee

Which statements assess the potential impact of Juan's dismissal on the organization?

Options:
1. The company's replacement for Juan may not have the same level of experience
2. The magazine's replacement for Juan may not attract as many clients
3. The magazine has no suitable replacements for Juan in case of his dismissal
4. The magazine's replacement for Juan may require a significant increase in salary

Answer

Option 1: This option is correct. Juan is a veteran photographer.

Option 2: This option is correct. Juan has been popular for his signature style of photos. His replacement would have to develop a unique style that may or may not draw in clients.

Option 3: This option is incorrect. Juan isn't the only photographer on the radar at the magazine. There are several people that could be potential replacements.

Option 4: This option is incorrect. Darlene noted that she could probably find a replacement photographer for Juan at half his salary.

Case Study: Question 3 of 3

What's the most appropriate decision for Darlene to make in regard to Juan?

Options:
1. She should take a day or two to make sure she wants to dismiss Juan and then do it promptly
2. She should keep Juan as the editorial photographer
3. She should give Juan an unprecedented second warning because of his potential
4. She should delay Juan's dismissal for six months until she's able to find and train a replacement
5. She should delay Juan's dismissal just for a week so that he can try again to revert to his old style

Answer

Option 1: This is the correct option. Juan has not made an effort to improve his photography as per expectations. Clients remain largely unhappy with his work.

Option 2: This option is incorrect. Juan did not change his style as requested, although he had the potential and mentoring to enable him to do so.

Option 3: This option is incorrect. Potential without effort is useless. Juan doesn't want to change and this may impact clients' decisions to use the magazine's services.

Option 4: This option is incorrect. Failure to dismiss Juan immediately would send a message that his behavior and performance are acceptable.

Option 5: This option is incorrect. There is no reason to prolong a dismissal by even a week without good reason like an exceptional personal situation.

SECTION 4 - PREPARING A DISMISSAL LETTER

SECTION 4 - Preparing a Dismissal Letter

Composing the dismissal letter is the final step in the process of preparing to dismiss an employee.

The dismissal letter should contain relevant names and dates, a clear description of the dismissal decision, information on what led to that decision, and evidence from witnesses. If all the essential information is included, just cause for dismissal is much less likely to be challenged.

ESSENTIAL ELEMENTS OF A DISMISSAL LETTER

Essential elements of a dismissal letter

Once you've ensured the employee knows the rules, have provided warnings, and have made your decision to go through with the dismissal, you should then write the dismissal letter. The dismissal letter will be given to the employee during the dismissal interview. A well-written dismissal letter informs the employee of the dismissal in writing, and it also helps you complete your personnel records. Plus, it helps support the dismissal in case of a dispute.

A well-written dismissal letter should contain five main elements: dates, names, a description of the dismissal decision, information on what led to the dismissal, and information on witnesses.

Dates

Enter the date of the dismissal letter itself near the top. Also include exact dates in the section containing information on what led to the dismissal.

The dates in an example of a Dismissal Letter include the date of the letter, March 2, as well as the dates of progressive discipline: February 9, February 18, February 24, and March 1.

Names

Include the name of the employee being dismissed at the top of the letter and the manager who is dismissing the employee at the bottom of the letter. Also, where possible, state the names of any witnesses involved in any part of the dismissal process.

The names in the example Dismissal Letter include the name of the employee, Mr. Omar Pines; names of the witnesses, Jane Carter and Beth Ortiz; and the name of the manager, Stephanie Rabinowitz.

Description of the dismissal decision

In a short opening paragraph consisting of one or two sentences, clearly state that the employee is being dismissed. You can also restate the dismissal decision in the closing paragraph.

The description of the dismissal decision is included both in the opening and closing paragraphs of the example Dismissal Letter.

The opening paragraph states: *"This letter is to inform you that you are being dismissed immediately for failure to comply with company-wide customer service standards."*

The closing paragraph uses these words: *"...I have no other choice but to dismiss you from your position immediately."*

Information on what led to the dismissal

After the description of the dismissal decision, detail what led to it. Include exact dates of offenses, progressive discipline, and corrective actions.

Information on what led to the dismissal is included in the body of the example Dismissal Letter. It states:

"On February 9, 20xx, you received a verbal warning for your poor customer service performance. On February 18, 20xx, you received a first written warning for continued customer service issues. On February 24, 20xx, you received a second and final written warning that reiterated your continued substandard customer service performance. In each of these instances, you acknowledged that you knew what was expected from you and you promised to improve. You were given until March 1, 20xx to make the agreed upon improvements.

During that time, you were asked to attend a workshop to help you improve your customer service skills. You declined. You also refused the support offered by one of your experienced colleagues, Jane Carter. Finally, you were rude to a customer yet again. Your supervisor, Beth Ortiz, witnessed the interaction, and the customer also reported it.

Your failure to comply with corrective actions, as well as your failure to properly interact with this customer shows an ongoing inability to perform at an acceptable level, as well as a lack of concern for your job."

Information on witnesses

Where applicable, include names of witnesses and their observations on the employee's inappropriate performance or behavior.

The example dismissal letter states that the employee refused the support offered by one Jane Carter – an experienced colleague. The employee's supervisor, Beth Ortiz, also witnessed the employee being rude to a customer.

CHAPTER 2 - MANAGING THE DISMISSAL OF AN EMPLOYEE

CHAPTER 2 - Managing the Dismissal of an Employee
 SECTION 1 - Preparing for the Dismissal Interview
 SECTION 2 - Conducting the Dismissal Interview
 SECTION 3 - Following up on the Dismissal

SECTION 1 - PREPARING FOR THE DISMISSAL INTERVIEW

SECTION 1 - Preparing for the Dismissal Interview

When preparing to conduct a dismissal interview, it's important to adopt the right mindset. This means being calm, treating the employee with respect, and being convinced that you're doing the right thing.

You should also be careful to ensure that the interview is correctly structured. If firing, the sequence of steps is to first state the decision, then allude to the steps of the disciplinary procedure, state when the dismissal takes effect, present the package and the company's reference policy, and then present the dismissal letter. If it's a layoff, the process is similar to a firing but the first two steps are replaced by three alternative steps: explain the situation truthfully, express gratitude, and provide encouragement and offer to assist where possible.

THE IMPORTANCE OF MANAGING DISMISSALS

The importance of managing dismissals

Imagine a scenario where a company lays off a number of employees. As workers see their colleagues being laid off, they become afraid for their own jobs and perhaps a little resentful. A company's efficiency and the morale of its staff can be negatively impacted, whether employees are being fired or laid off.

The quality of the company's products may suffer as a result. There may be damage to the company's image and reputation, and what was supposed to benefit the company by cutting costs ends up being very costly. This type of situation can be avoided by managing the dismissals of employees effectively.

Practical benefits of managing dismissals effectively

As you may have noted, effectively managing a dismissal results in the preservation of the employee's dignity. It also helps to maintain positive work relationships within the employee's team and to maintain or improve the quality and productivity of the organization. Managing dismissals also helps to preserve the organization's image.

THE DISMISSAL INTERVIEW

The dismissal interview

Dismissing an employee will inevitably involve a conversation with the employee concerned. This conversation is referred to as a dismissal interview, and if you have to conduct one, it's important that you're properly prepared. There are three steps to managing a dismissal effectively. First you need to prepare for the dismissal interview. Then you must conduct the interview with the employee in the correct way. And finally, you need to remember to follow up on the dismissal appropriately.

Employees may leave a company voluntarily – such as when they resign or retire – or involuntarily – through dismissal. Dismissals occur for a variety of reasons. The two main reasons are firing and laying off. In both cases employees are going to lose their jobs, but when a company is doing layoffs, the employees aren't at fault. Managers may therefore find dismissal interviews even more difficult in these cases.

Dismissal interviews will vary according to the situation. But there are some common characteristics for effectively handling a dismissal interview:

- the meeting should be short in duration,
- the meeting should take place in private,
- state clearly exactly why the employee is being dismissed and when the dismissal takes place, and
- it shouldn't come as a surprise to the employee.

Short in duration

Dismissal meetings are ideally short in duration – 10 to 15 minutes is usually sufficient. This will help to ensure that you stick to the point. Preparing beforehand can help you do this.

Take place in private

The interview should take place in private as this helps to ensure that the dignity of the employee is preserved. But it may help to have a witness present in some situations if you perceive the employee might subsequently commence legal action. You must also stick to the facts but try to empathize with the employee, and don't be too clinical or cold in your approach.

State when dismissal takes place

During the interview, it should be explained exactly why the employee is being dismissed and from when the dismissal is effective. In the case of a layoff, this may involve explaining the company's challenges. In the case of a firing, you should remind the employee about the actions taken as part of a disciplinary procedure prior to the dismissal and for example past warnings about misconduct or poor performance.

Shouldn't come as a surprise

A dismissal announcement ought not to come as a surprise. In the case of a layoff, the company's intention to cut staff numbers should have been announced prior to a dismissal interview. In the case of firing, the employee should have already been put on notice for performance or behavioral shortcomings.

Although a dismissal will be difficult for employees, there are guidelines you should follow to ensure the news of a layoff or firing doesn't present too big a shock to the employee or negatively impact the company. When laying off an employee, the manager should be sure to communicate the organizational strategy to employees prior to the dismissal interview. Try to be honest and transparent about what may happen at that point.

In the case of a firing, the manager should ensure prior to the dismissal interview that a progressive disciplinary process has been followed. If the issue is poor performance, the dismissal interview shouldn't be the first time the employee is made aware of this. You should have documentation proving that the employee received notice of subpar performance at previous performance appraisals. You should also be able to show that the person was given opportunities and help to improve.

Question

Which statements describe good practice in relation to dismissal interviews?

Options:

1. The dismissal interview is short in duration
2. The dismissal interview takes place in private
3. In the case of a layoff, the manager has informed employees of the company's strategy in advance
4. If the employee is being fired, it should generally take place after a progressive disciplinary procedure
5. Employees should be told about other employees' situations during the interview
6. The dismissal interview should be handled in a business-like, clinical manner

7. The interview should state the date from which the dismissal is effective

Answer

Option 1: This option is correct. A dismissal interview should ideally be no more than 10 to 15 minutes. Option 2: This option is correct. To preserve the employee's dignity, a dismissal interview should be in

private. If necessary, however, it may include one witness.

Option 3: This option is correct. It's important that a layoff doesn't come as a surprise in a dismissal interview.

Option 4: This option is correct. Employees should receive warnings about their conduct or subpar performance before being dismissed.

Option 5: This option is incorrect. All dismissal interviews should be private and handled on an individual basis.

Option 6: This option is incorrect. While it's important to stick to facts, you should also try to empathize with the employee being dismissed.

Option 7: This option is correct. It's important to be clear and decisive by informing when the dismissal is effective.

PREPARING FOR DISMISSAL INTERVIEWS

Preparing for dismissal interviews

In order to manage a dismissal effectively, it's critical that you prepare well. Before the dismissal interview takes place, you need to ensure you're adequately prepared by adopting the right mindset and preparing the structure of the interview.

Here are some general principles to help ensure you're in the right frame of mind for the dismissal interview. First, be calm; don't conduct the interview when angry or upset. Second, remember to treat employees with respect and allow them to keep their dignity. Putting yourself in their position and not discussing the dismissal with others before the interview will help you follow this guideline. Third, be confident in your reasons. Even if it's a layoff, you can be clear that there's no other option, while still expressing sincere regret.

You also need to ensure that the dismissal interview is properly structured. This structure will differ a little depending on whether it's a case of firing or laying off an employee. If you're firing an employee, here's how to structure the interview:
1. state the dismissal decision at the beginning of the meeting,
2. allude to the steps of the disciplinary procedure already taken to emphasize that this isn't a snap decision,
3. state when the dismissal takes effect – you should decide this beforehand,
4. present information regarding the severance package, if any, or benefit entitlements,
5. present the company's reference policy by explaining the parts of the company policy manual that relate to firing, and
6. provide the employee with a dismissal letter containing a concise explanation of the relevant facts.

State the decision

Dismissing an Employee

You should try to impart the news of the firing quickly, professionally, and sensitively. It may help to jot down some notes beforehand to help you stay focused. It's important to do this calmly and empathetically.

Allude to disciplinary procedure
Because the employee is being fired, you need to refer to the disciplinary steps the company has already taken. This may be previous performance appraisals or misconduct warnings. The dismissal shouldn't come as a surprise.

State when the dismissal takes effect
You need to have worked out in advance when the date of dismissal will be. In the case of firing, the dismissal is often effective immediately. You need to state this.

Present severance package
You should present the elements of the employee's severance package or any relevant entitlements they may have.

Present the reference policy
Ensure that you're aware of the company's reference policy in advance of the meeting and explain it clearly to the employee.

Provide dismissal letter
You should have the dismissal letter ready before the meeting. Ensure there's no misunderstanding about why employees have been fired before they leave the meeting.

Consider this example. Bridget is the manager of a financial services company. It's come to her attention that one of the company's employees, Mark, continued to give advice to a client based on privileged information, which is against company policy. Mark received a written warning a month ago. However, he has ignored the warning. Bridget has therefore decided to terminate his employment.

Follow along as Bridget conducts the dismissal interview with Mark.

Bridget: Hello, Mark. I've called this meeting to inform you that unfortunately we've made the decision to end your employment with the company.

Bridget says calmly

Mark: Really? Wow, I'm shocked. Why?

Bridget: You were presented with a written warning last month regarding your conduct in relation to illegally advising a client based on privileged information. As your conduct hasn't changed since this warning, we have no choice but to terminate your contract. For legal reasons, this needs to be effective immediately.

Mark: OK, well, this is a huge shock. I hope you're aware that I'm not the only employee who's been doing this. Are you firing Mary too?

Mark says angrily

Bridget: I'm afraid I can't discuss other employees' situations with you. I do want to let you know that you're still entitled to exercise your share options within the time permitted. I'd also like to provide you with a copy of our reference policy and this dismissal letter. Please feel free to ask me any questions you may have.

If you have to lay off an employee, here's how you should structure the dismissal interview: state the decision by explaining the situation truthfully, express gratitude for the employee's work, outline positive prospects for job seeking, state when the dismissal takes effect, outline the reference policy, present the severance package, and finally provide the dismissal letter.

First, try to be truthful. People want to know the truth about why they're being laid off. It will help to reduce their aggravation if they feel they're being treated with dignity and respect.

Second, you should express gratitude for the employees' hard work, especially as they've done nothing wrong. You should then move from the negative by providing encouragement and offering to assist where possible. Aim to inspire them and leave things on a good note.

Then continue with the remaining steps of the process by stating when the dismissal takes effect, present the reference policy, then the severance package, and finally the dismissal letter.

Question Set

To prepare for a dismissal interview, you need to ensure you adopt the right attitude and that you structure the meeting appropriately.

Question 1 of 2

Which statements describe how you should prepare for a dismissal interview effectively?

Options:

1. Ensure that you're calm and don't conduct the interview when angry or upset
2. Aim to preserve the dignity of the employees by putting yourself in their position
3. Aim to be confident in the reasons for the dismissal
4. Tell other employees about the dismissal plans
5. Adopt a clinical approach to the dismissal

Answer

Option 1: This option is correct. It's important to be calm to ensure you adopt the right mindset for the interview.

Option 2: This option is correct. It's important to prepare by thinking about the situation from the employee's point of view.

Option 3: This option is correct. To adopt the right mindset for the interview, you need to convince yourself of the reasons for dismissal.

Option 4: This option is incorrect. To preserve the employee's dignity, you shouldn't tell others about the dismissal before the interview.

Option 5: This option is incorrect. It's important to empathize while sticking to the point of the interview.

Question 2 of 2

Which statements describe the correct structure of a dismissal interview?

Options:

1. When firing, you should state the decision first, then allude to the steps of the disciplinary procedure, state when it takes effect, present the package and the reference policy, and then provide the dismissal letter

2. In a layoff dismissal interview, you should start by explaining the situation truthfully, thanking the employee, providing encouragement and assistance if possible, and then proceed with the final four steps of the firing procedure

3. When firing an employee, you should act immediately to name her publicly, inform her of the decision, and send a dismissal letter after the meeting

4. When laying off, you should thank the employee for his work and prolong the meeting so that he feels more respected before telling him the truth

Answer

Option 1: This option is correct. This is the correct sequence of steps for dismissal if the employee is being fired.

Option 2: This option is correct. There are a three steps in a layoff dismissal that replace the first two steps of the firing process.

Option 3: This option is incorrect. You shouldn't tell anyone of the dismissal before the interview and the statement skips a few steps of the correct firing process.

Option 4: This option is incorrect. You should tell the truth from the beginning, thank the employee, and then provide encouragement and assistance where possible.

SECTION 2 - CONDUCTING THE DISMISSAL INTERVIEW

SECTION 2 - Conducting the Dismissal Interview

There are some guidelines you can refer to make the task of conducting dismissal interviews less daunting. First, remember to show compassion and empathy toward the employee being dismissed throughout the interview. Second, always be in control of the conversation, and third, try to be honest and help the employee understand the reasons for the dismissal. Fourth, while remaining empathetic, be sure to be decisive throughout the interview and not respond to any questions you feel are inappropriate. And finally, don't react to negative feedback on the spot, even if you feel angry or upset, but rather try to reiterate the reasons and move on with the interview.

When conducting a dismissal interview it's important to state the decision quickly and sensitively. Remember to be empathetic and preserve the employee's dignity. You should spend a short time helping the employee understand the reasons by asking specific questions and not being personally critical.

You shouldn't respond to negative feedback by getting annoyed or discussing false accusations. You should instead briefly reiterate the reason and politely move on with the meeting. It's important to be decisive by not answering inappropriate questions, not entering into negotiation with the employee and by stating that the decision is final.

GUIDELINES FOR INTERVIEW

Guidelines for interview

Conducting a dismissal interview can be a daunting task. But there are some principles that can help. The first guideline is to show compassion and empathy toward the employee being dismissed throughout the interview. Second, aim to always be in control of the conversation. Third, try to be honest and help the employee understand the reasons for the dismissal. Fourth, while remaining empathetic, be sure to be decisive throughout the interview. And finally, don't react to negative feedback on the spot.

Whether the dismissal is a lay off or a firing, it's always appropriate to empathize with the employee. Part of showing compassion and empathy is stating the decision early on in the meeting, so that the employee isn't kept in a state of anxiety or confusion about the reason for the meeting.

Even if the employee is being dismissed due to misconduct or performance issues, it's still important to remember the employee's right to be treated with dignity and compassion.

If you're unsure about how to handle a dismissal empathetically, there are a few tips you can consider: Think carefully in advance about what you're going to say so that you can be as tactful as possible, state the decision quickly but sensitively, and give honest reasons for the dismissal.

Think carefully in advance

To ensure that you handle the dismissal interview with empathy and compassion, it helps to think carefully about what you're going to say in advance of the interview.

State decision quickly but sensitively

When it comes to the time of the interview, state the decision quickly and professionally but in an empathetic and sensitive manner.

Give honest reasons for dismissal

To avoid the employee feeling patronized, give honest reasons for the dismissal as well as feedback and advice where appropriate.

As well as being empathetic and showing compassion, you should try to be in control throughout the interview. This means remaining calm and defusing emotional outbursts by maintaining a calm tone.

Peter, the manager of a large corporate department, is conducting a dismissal interview with Martina, an employee who is being laid-off. Follow the conversation as Peter shows compassion during the interview while remaining in control.

Peter: Hello Martina, I've asked you along today to inform you that sadly, due to economic pressure on the firm's resources we have no choice but to downsize our work force and we're going to have to let you go, I'm afraid.

Martina: Oh this is quite shocking, I knew that the firm was planning to lay-off staff but had hoped I would make the cut.

Peter: Yes, I can understand that you would have hoped that and believe me, we've tried everything to make it possible to hold on to you as you've been an excellent employee. However, the firm has a last in first out policy in these circumstances and you've been with us for a shorter period than some other employees.

Martina: It's a pity that the firm has this policy I thought I had a future here, I feel quite upset about this.

Peter: I thought you did too, Martina, and this is a regrettable situation. I will do everything I can to help you get employment elsewhere. I have a few contacts I can give an excellent reference to on your behalf.

Martina: I appreciate your honesty and your advice, Peter.

Peter successfully managed this dismissal interview by preparing his approach in advance. He made sure he knew Martina's history with the firm. To ensure he was compassionate, he prepared how to deliver the news tactfully but quickly.

He is empathetic by offering his advice and support for finding a new job.

Although he's compassionate, Peter remains calm and in control even when Martina expresses her disappointment about the decision.

Question

What statements demonstrate how a manager can show compassion and empathy toward dismissed employees whilst remaining in control?

Options:

1. Be honest about the reasons for their dismissal and offer feedback

2. State the decision quickly and as painlessly as possible in a professional but sensitive manner

3. If the employee becomes emotional, try to maintain a calm tone and defuse the tension

Dismissing an Employee

4. Show a lot of empathy toward laid-off employees but little toward fired employees as it's their own fault

5. Be honest about the reasons for the dismissal but if they become emotional, try to adapt your explanation to make it easier for them

Answer

Option 1: This option is correct. By empathizing and being honest about the reasons, employees won't feel humiliated or patronized.

Option 2: This option is correct. It's preferable to get to the point quickly but sensitively to avoid any unnecessary discomfort for either party.

Option 3: This option is incorrect. The most compassionate way to handle an emotional outburst is to remain calm and in control and try to defuse the situation.

Option 4: This option is incorrect. It's true that laid-off employees are less responsible for losing their jobs than fired employees, but all dismissed employees deserve compassion in the interview.

Option 5: This option is incorrect. If you've prepared properly, you'll have prepared the most tactful way to present the reasons honestly so that you can be empathetic and remain in control.

It's important for both the company and employees' dignity that you're honest and help them understand the reasons for the dismissal. Try to make eye contact with the employee as you present the reasons.

In addition to being honest about the reasons for the dismissal, try to help the employee to understand them. The best way to do this is to avoid direct criticism as this leads to a defensive attitude. Instead ask carefully selected questions that will lead the employee himself to talk about what went wrong.

While it's important to answer employee concerns, there will inevitably be some questions that you're unable to answer. For instance, if an employee asks questions that have legal ramifications for you or the company or if they ask a question that you simply feel is inappropriate, you shouldn't make an attempt to answer it.

Another guideline for conducting effective interviews is to be decisive. Try to avoid a situation where the employee attempts to negotiate or believe that they can do something to change your mind. Inform them that the decision is final and not subject to change.

Question

Which statements exemplify following best practice in helping an employee understand and being decisive during a dismissal interview?

Options:

1. "How do you think it affects the discipline of other employees when you keep turning up late despite repeated warnings for this misconduct?"

2. "I cannot answer a question regarding the pay or employment status of another employee so please don't ask"

3. "I'm not willing to negotiate, the decision is final I'm afraid and effective immediately"

4. "I'm not willing to discuss the reasons you're fired and it's final I'm afraid"

5. "I know this may come as a shock but I'm laying you off, it's not my decision I wanted to keep you on really but management say you have to go"

Answer

Option 1: This option is correct. Asking a question is a good way to help an employee understand the reasons behind their dismissal by encouraging them to answer it for themselves.

Option 2: This option is correct. When helping the employee understand, answer the employee's questions if you can, but be firm about the questions you cannot answer.

Option 3: This option is correct. It's important to help the employee understand the reasons for dismissal but also to ensure you're not lured into negotiation.

Option 4: This option is incorrect. It's important to be decisive during dismissals but also to help employees understand the reasons for their dismissal by explaining or asking questions.

Option 5: This option is incorrect. It's important to be honest with the employee in the reasons for the dismissal, shirking the blame elsewhere doesn't help them understand why they're being let go.

The last guideline is don't react to negative feedback on the spot. Dismissed employees may become emotional or even abusive. While it's important to allow time to reflect on any negative or abusive feedback after the event, it's critical that you try not to react to it during the meeting.

Some managers will be tempted to react to negative feedback as they may become emotional themselves or hurt by comments made. It's normal to feel for the person being dismissed, it shows that you weighed up the decision and didn't make it lightly.

However, it's important to have confidence in the decision you made and not enter into an argument by reacting to negativity.

Nancy is the managing director of a medium sized retail store. She's conducting a dismissal interview with Brenda, who's being laid off. Follow the conversation as Nancy demonstrates the principles of being honest, being decisive, and avoiding the temptation to respond to negative feedback on the spot.

Nancy: So that brings us to the end of our interview. Are there any questions I can answer for you, Brenda?

Dismissing an Employee

Brenda: I don't think this is fair Nancy, after all the years I've put in here. How can you do this to me? It's grossly unfair.

Nancy: I understand that you're upset, Brenda but I've explained that we had no other choice. I've had to let a lot of other employees go who've also put in a lot of work here. It's for the reasons I've explained that the company can't afford to keep on part-time staff any longer.

Brenda: Who else are you letting go? I don't believe the reasons you're giving me. You never liked me, and you never helped me to be anything other than a part-time employee here.

Nancy: Brenda, what you're saying is untrue. This isn't personal at all. I cannot discuss other employees' situations either, as I'm sure you'll understand that's confidential. I'd like to part on good terms and help you any way I can to get a new job. But I'll have to bring this meeting to a close and give you your dismissal letter.

Nancy effectively handles Brenda's negative feedback by not reacting to it on the spot. She reassures her calmly that her beliefs about it being personal are untrue and then she moves on.

Nancy is honest with Brenda about the reasons for her dismissal and helps her to understand them as best she can. She's also decisive with Brenda by explaining that she can't answer questions she feels are inappropriate about other employees' situations.

Question

What statements would be appropriate responses during a dismissal interview to an employee accusing you of unfair treatment?

Options:

1. "I'm sorry you feel this is personal, but this is purely a business decision based on the reasons I've explained to you"
2. "I can assure you that this is not personal, I've explained the reasons we've come to this decision and I'll have to move on with the interview I'm afraid"
3. "How can you accuse me of that? I've always looked out for you, I'm really upset you could even suggest such a thing"
4. "That's a ridiculous statement, you know you've made me do this and I'm so angry you have the cheek to try to make me feel bad about it"

Answer

Option 1: This option is correct. Assuming you've helped the employee understand the reasons already, don't react to negative feedback and reiterate the business reasons for the dismissal if necessary.

Option 2: This option is correct. It's important to remain in control by not reacting to negative feedback and try to steer the meeting forward.

Option 3: This option is incorrect. Despite how you may feel, it's best not to become emotional yourself and react to negative comments but you can still be empathetic.

Option 4: This option is incorrect. It's natural that you may feel angry if an employee blames you and makes you feel bad but you shouldn't show this or react to negative feedback in the interview.

SECTION 3 - FOLLOWING UP ON THE DISMISSAL

SECTION 3 - Following up on the Dismissal

After a dismissal has taken place, it's critical that managers follow up on the dismissal effectively. First you should follow up with the employee. If the employee was laid-off, offer support and a positive reference if company policy allows. If the dismissal was a firing, you may also decide to provide a reference. Agree with the employee how you can explain the reasons as a learning experience.

Second, it's important to manage the impact of the dismissal on the team and on the organization as a whole. Be honest and open about the dismissal and avoid speaking ill of the dismissed employee.

FOLLOW UP WITH EMPLOYEE

Follow up with employee

Although each dismissal interview will vary according to the situation, it's possible to use guidelines to navigate through it with confidence and professionalism. Conducting an interview is something that every manager will have to do at some point. Experience and practice will help you to improve your effective handling of dismissals each time you conduct one.

After preparing for the dismissal and then conducting the dismissal interview, the last step in the process is following up on the dismissal.

There are two aspects to appropriately following up on a dismissal. You need to follow up with the employee, and you need to manage the impact of the dismissal on the team and the organization. The first step in the process is to follow up with the employee. The approach you take will be slightly different depending on whether the employee is being laid off or fired.

When laying off, you should try to provide the employee with additional support. This could be in the form of advice and references for getting another job.

In the case of both fired and laid off employees, you'll need to agree during the dismissal interview whether or not you'll be providing a reference. You should also agree on the content of the reference to avoid potential problems in the future. Since dismissal due to a layoff is not the result of poor performance or misconduct, it's good practice to provide a positive reference to help employees' chances of finding alternative employment.

It's possible that you'll be unsure about whether to provide a reference and what to include in it, particularly in the case of a firing. When deciding about whether or not to give a reference, you need to be aware if your company has a policy on this. Also, if you are intending to give a reference, you might want to talk to the employee about what to put in the reference.

In general, for dismissals there are two things to consider regarding the issue of references.

Be aware of company policy

Some employers have a policy of not providing references for dismissed employees, regardless of whether they were laid off or fired. Others will provide references for laid-off employees but not for firings. Whatever your company's policy is, you should state it clearly to the employee. Keep in mind if there are issues that might be critically important to employees carrying out their job safely, you could be legally obligated to disclose this information to their next employer. Seek legal advice in this case.

Talk to the employee about the reference

Another option is to discuss with the employee what you might put into the reference, if you're providing one. Many people know that their dismissal isn't personal, and treat it as a learning experience. Even if it's a firing due to poor performance, you can agree with the employee what you could include in the reference that describes the event honestly but as a positive learning experience. It's important not to be dishonest but you don't need to document each and every detail either, if it's not pertinent to their ability to do a job safely and competently.

Question

Which statements describe following up effectively with employees after dismissal?

Options:

1. A manager provides a laid off employee with advice on seeking a new job
2. A manager refuses a fired employee's request for a dishonest reference
3. A manager consults his company's reference policy when firing an employee
4. To avoid confrontation, a manager gives a fired employee a dishonest reference to appease her following a difficult interview
5. A manager gives a fired employee a truthful reference, listing everything she did wrong in detail to help her learn from mistakes

Answer

Option 1: This option is correct. It's helpful to provide laid off employees with advice to help them find alternative employment.

Option 2: This option is correct. If you provide a dishonest reference you could be held legally liable for damage that employee causes in his next workplace.

Option 3: This option is correct. It's important to know the reference policy. A company might give no references, give references only to laid off employees, or decide on a case by case basis.

Option 4: This option is incorrect. It's not advisable to give dishonest references as you can be held liable by future employers for damages done by a referred employee.

Option 5: This option is incorrect. If providing a reference to a fired employee, it's better to state it as a positive learning experience without listing all mistakes in detail.

MANAGE THE IMPACT

Manage the impact

It's important to manage the impact of the dismissal on other employees and on the organization. Dismissals can have a major impact on the team and on the organization as a whole. As a manager, you should follow two guidelines to make sure positive and productive work relationships are maintained within the team: be honest and open, and avoid speaking badly of the dismissed employee.

Laying off or firing an employee may have a negative effect on the employees who remain. It's important that you're open and honest with the other members of the team about the dismissal. One worry for managers after dismissals is that other employees will leave as a result. If the person was fired due to misconduct or poor performance, the reasons are often obvious to other team members. In these cases you should still be open about the dismissal to clear the air.

The dismissal might present an opportunity to review with your remaining team how processes and procedures are carried out and to clarify expectations. This will also help to retain valued employees after a dismissal.

Consider this example. The manager of a transport company recently fired a driver due to misconduct. He arranges to meet with the other drivers to discuss what's happened. He explains that the employee has been dismissed. One employee asks why and the manager explains that he broke the rules of the company on a number occasions.

Most of the team members already understand the reasons for the firing. The manager then explains how much he values their hard work, thanks them for their support, and asks for any suggestions they might have for improvements.

Question

Which statements represent appropriate follow up with other employees after a dismissal?

Options:

1. A meeting is held with remaining employees to inform them about the dismissal
2. The dismissal is used as an opportunity to review processes and procedures with remaining employees
3. A manager chats with employees about the unpleasant characteristics of a fired employee to boost their morale
4. A leader explains the personal circumstances of a dismissed employee to other employees because she wants to be seen as honest

Answer

Option 1: This option is correct. Remaining employees are more likely to stay if you're honest about the dismissal.

Option 2: This option is correct. It helps to retain employees if you seek to improve the work environment by reviewing processes after a dismissal.

Option 3: This option is incorrect. It's important to be open and honest with remaining employees but not to speak badly of the dismissed employee.

Option 4: This option is incorrect. You should be honest about the actual dismissal without disclosing personal or confidential information.

The second guideline to keep in mind when managing the impact of a dismissal is avoid speaking badly of the dismissed employee. Speaking badly of these employees, such as giving reasons why you disliked them personally, will make remaining employees wonder about what you say behind their backs.

Consider this example. A manager at a coffee shop recently laid off some employees. This decision was necessary. However, many of the staff members, including the manager, didn't get along with one of the dismissed employees.

When the manager meets with the employees, he's open and honest about the dismissals and explains that they were unavoidable. When one of the employees says how annoying one of the dismissed employees was, the manager states that speaking ill of absent employees isn't encouraged in the workplace.

Ensure you follow any legal advice given to you from appropriate company representatives both before and after a dismissal. Dismissing employees is a hard but important lesson in leadership. Every time you conduct a dismissal, you'll likely learn more about yourself and the nature of people in general.

Question

Which statements represent examples of effectively managing the impact of dismissals on the organization?

Options:

Dismissing an Employee

1. After a dismissal a manager makes it clear to the remaining team that speaking badly of the dismissed employee isn't encouraged
2. A manager reassures remaining employees after laying-off an employee that she'll help to ease the transition
3. A manager ensures to follow legal advice before making a decision to dismiss an employee
4. A manager tells a fellow manager that he had his own reasons for firing an employee who worked on each of their teams and refuses to explain why
5. Following a lay-off, a manager states to the team that the dismissed employees were no use and stupid

Answer

Option 1: This option is correct. It's important to talk with remaining employees about the dismissal and discourage speaking badly about the dismissed employee.

Option 2: This option is correct. It's good practice to help and reassure managers who also worked with dismissed employees.

Option 3: This option is correct. If in any doubt about your company's position in dismissing an employee, it's important to seek legal advice before and after a dismissal.

Option 4: This option is incorrect. Part of a manager's job is to reassure and help fellow managers in the organization after a dismissal.

Option 5: This option is incorrect. Despite personal feelings, managers should avoid badmouthing after a dismissal.

REFERENCES

References

The Management Bible - 2005, Nelson, Bob and Economy, Peter, John Wiley & Sons

The Manager's Guide to HR: Hiring, Firing, Performance Evaluations, Documentation, Benefits, and Everything Else You Need to Know - 2009, Muller, Max, AMACOM

Letting People Go: The People-Centered Approach to Firing and Laying Off Employees - 2010, Matt Schlosberg, Business Expert Express

GLOSSARY

Glossary

C

corrective actions - Actions employees can take to correct their behavioral or performance issues.

M

major offense - An inappropriate behavioral or performance issue in the workplace that causes harm to employees or the company and usually warrants immediate dismissal.

mentoring - A mutually beneficial relationship in which an experienced person, such as a manager, guides a coworker, sharing experiences and imparting knowledge and confidence.

minor offense - An inappropriate behavioral or performance issue in the workplace that doesn't cause immediate harm to employees or the company, but can lead to bigger problems. Minor offenses usually warrant progressive discipline and corrective actions before a dismissal takes place.

O

offenses - Inappropriate behavioral or performance issues in the workplace. An offense can be categorized by severity as a major offense or a minor offense, and may give cause for dismissal.

P

performance review - A mechanism for regular discussion and evaluation of an employee's job performance. Performance reviews are often one- on-one discussions between a manager and a subordinate, and cover quantifiable job responsibilities.

progressive discipline - A system of discipline where the severity of the disciplinary actions increase in relation to the nature and continuation of the offense.

www.ingramcontent.com/pod-product-compliance
Lightning Source LLC
Chambersburg PA
CBHW020709180526
45163CB00008B/3013